PRAYER
The Eastern Tradition

Andrew Ryder, SCJ

Edited by
THOMAS CURRAN

LIVING FLAME PRESS
BOX 74 LOCUST VALLEY, N.Y. 11560

Contents

Prayer
and
Theology

St. Thomas Aquinas once said that it is easier for a peasant to become a saint than it is for a theologian and at the end of his life he described his immense literary output as straw compared to the reality of God. This attitude of the great medieval thinker is often reflected and distorted at the popular level in an actual dismissal of theology as unnecessary to union with God. Even worse, theology is seen as an obstacle to divine union.

Such a misunderstanding of theology hardly does justice to the mystical tradition of the Church. At its best the study of the Christian mysteries has never isolated them from a life of prayer and contemplation and the Church both in the East and in the West gives powerful witness to the need for blending theology and prayer: one without the other is undesirable.

"None of the mysteries of the most secret wisdom of God ought to appear alien or altogether transcendent to us, but in all humility we must apply our spirit to the contemplation of divine things," wrote the Metropolitan Philaret of Moscow over a century ago.[1] In the East there is no sharp distinction between prayer and theology. Far from being divorced they are seen as supporting and completing each other. One is impossible without the other. Without a sound theology the Orthodox fear that prayer could become a personal experience deprived of any certainty, an illusion. But, even more importantly, without a basis in prayer, theological speculation would easily remain isolated from life. Theology is not an end in itself, but rather a means, a way to union with God.

The first centuries of the Christian Church witness a continual battle to safeguard sound theology: "God became man that men might become gods." Union with God, the goal of prayer, was at the heart of those early conflicts. The doctrine of the Trinity, so much lost sight of in the Western Church as the basis of piety, was central to the struggle. But, as defined by the ecumenical councils, it has retained its place as the foundation of the spirituality of the Orthodox Church. It is here that we can learn most from their tradition.

Western theology has stressed the unity of God's nature and gone from an analysis of the divine nature to the consideration of the three persons. This has been the common approach in the West since the middle ages and it is classically exposed in the *Summa* of St. Thomas Aquinas. The influence of the method on prayer, however, reveals both the intimate link between theology and prayer and the weakness of the method. Commenting on the outcome Rahner has written: "Despite their orthodox confession of the Trinity, Christians are, in their practical life, almost mere 'monotheists.' We must be willing to admit that, should the doctrine of the Trinity have to be dropped as false, the major part of religious literature could well remain virtually unchanged." Even the doctrine of the Incarnation, continues Rahner, is insufficiently trinitarian in terms of everyday piety. "Other areas of theology, too, pay insufficient attention to the real theology of the Trinity, e.g. Eucharistic theology (when it indicates that the sacrifice of the Mass is offered to the three divine persons in the same manner) and the theology of grace (which is described as a participation in the divine *nature* leading to a blessed vision of the divine *essence* — in the famous constitution of Benedict XII on the beatific vision there is no mention of the Trinity at all."[2]

In the East, on the other hand, the theological stress has been on the persons: Father, Son and Holy Spirit. The "economic" Trinity (the Trinity revealing itself in history) is the basis of their theology and their prayer. "Between the Trinity and hell there lies no other choice" said Lossky, and the starkness of the choice is a vivid reminder to us of the central tenet of Christian faith. In eastern eyes belief in the Trinity and prayerful reflection on the mystery are not luxuries reserved for a few specialists but are rather the framework on which personal and liturgical spirituality are developed.

That eastern theology judges our piety to be exclusively centred on Jesus is clearly shown in the following quotation from one of their leading writers:

"The personal relationship of man to the living God is no longer a relationship to the Trinity, but rather has as its object the person of Christ, who reveals to us the divine nature. Christian life and thought become christocentric, relying primarily upon the humanity of the incarnate Word; one might almost say that it is this which becomes their anchor of salvation." In the Orthodox Church, however, the doctrine of the Trinity is the unshakeable foundation of all religious thought, of all piety, of all spiritual life, of all experience.[3]

Mystical Theology

Theology, as the word itself indicates, means the study of God and hence it is never unrelated to the Trinity. But to attain knowledge and union with the divine persons it is necessary to pass beyond created things. It is only by way of abstraction and negation that one can hope to reach the transcendant. The way of negation, therefore, plays an important role in eastern prayer. By progressively eliminating all created knowledge it seeks to surpass the limits of understanding "imparting to the ignorance of what God is in His inaccessible nature the value of a mystical knowledge superior to the intellect."[4]

This mystical theology is elaborated in a short treatise which has played a considerable role in the subsequent development of Orthodox theology and spirituality: *The Nature of Mystical Theology* by Dionysius the Areopagite. The work is comprised of only five short chapters but its significance and influence are in inverse proportion to its size.

Although he tried to pass himself off as a disciple of St. Paul (Dionysius the Areopagite of Acts 17:16-34) the author could not have lived before the fifth century since the liturgy of the Mass he describes contains the *Credo*, an element not introduced until 476 A.D. Furthermore, there are no references to him in the Christian literature of the first five centuries and considering the impact he later made such neglect is inexplicable if he did indeed write before the sixth century.

Four major works are attributed to Dionysius. The first three differ in method from the one on mystical theology. *The Celestial Hierarchy* deals with the realm of the heavenly spirits, their nature, properties and division. The sevenfold order of angels given there has been the accepted one ever since. *The Ecclesiastical Hierarchy* treats the Church as the image of the world of heavenly spirits, with similar divisions of sacraments and orders. *The Divine Names* is a scriptural commentary on the names of God found in the Bible and Dionysius uses these names to explain the nature and attributes of God. All three books are in the tradition of positive theology and proceed by way of affirmation. Such an approach, says Dionysius, leads us to a knowledge of God, but it is imperfect. The surer way, the only real way to gain knowledge of God is by negation because created understanding, by its very nature, falls infinitely short of the divine being. Consequently, in his fourth and final work Dionysius adopts the negative stance.

The first chapter of *The Nature of Mystical Theology* begins with a prayer to the Holy Trinity. Dionysius asks to be guided "to the supreme height of mystical writings, which is beyond what is known, where the mysteries of theology, simple, unconditional, invariable, are laid bare in a darkness of silence beyond the light." The reader is invited to mystical contemplation and the renunciation of sensible and intellectual knowledge so that in perfect ignorance He who is above all knowledge may be apprehended. A process of purification is necessary: everything must be left behind as one scales the heights where God dwells.

The mystical ascent is compared to Moses' climb of Mount Sinai to meet Yahweh. This comparison goes back to Philo of Alexandria and was a favorite symbol of the Greek Fathers for God's otherness. Gregory of Nyssa, in his *Life of Moses*, has shown how Mount Sinai symbolises a way of contemplation superior to Moses' first encounter with God in the burning bush. Then Moses saw God in the brightness of flame; now He enters the darkness of the cloud, leaving behind all that can be seen or known. It is in the darkness of unknowing that he finds God.[5]

In Dionysius' first chapter Moses begins by purifying himself and putting aside all that is unclean. Then he hears "the many notes of the trumpets, he sees the many lights which flash forth many pure rays; then he is separated from the many, and with the chosen priests he reaches the heights of the divine ascent." Yet even on Mount Sinai Moses does not contemplate God, but rather the place where He dwells. So he passes into a state of mystical darkness and, shutting out all intelligible impressions, reaches the Unseen through an act of self-surrender. The negative way, therefore, is not one of intellectual consideration but rather a path to mystical union with

God who remains essentially incomprehensible to us.

The second chapter of *Mystical Theology* distinguishes and opposes the affirmative way of theology and the negative. Affirmative theology (followed by Dionysius in his first three works) is the way of *descent* from the higher realms of being to the lower. We come down from God through the divine names to His attributes. Negative theology, on the other hand, works *upwards*. As the sculptor cuts away all that disfigures the beauty of his statue so the person intent on God must put aside all that impedes him from divine union. It is because he is now following the more perfect way, the way of negation, writes Dionysius in the third chapter, that his present work is the shortest of his books. The negative way is one of few words.

Chapters four and five of the treatise, with their insistence that God is completely beyond all sensible and spiritual apprehension, takes negative theology to its ultimate limit. Enumerating and rejecting a whole series of attributes Dionysius says that God is neither potency, nor light; He neither lives nor is life; He is neither substance, nor time, nor knowledge, nor truth, neither kingdom, nor wisdom, neither one nor unity, neither divinity nor goodness. By the use of extreme paradox Dionysius concludes that God evades negation as well as affirmation: "When we make affirmation and negations about the things which are inferior to it, we affirm and deny nothing about the Cause itself, which, being wholly apart from all things, is above all affirmation, as the supremacy of Him who, being in His simplicity freed from all

14

things and beyond everything, is above all denial."

The negative (apophatic) method outlined by Dionysius constitutes a major characteristic of the eastern Church's theological tradition. Lossky stresses that it must be carefully distinguished from the neoplatonism of Plotinus, even though there are striking resemblances between the two. The God of Plotinus is not incomprehensible by nature; the God of Dionysius is. He is absolutely and radically unknowable. He is neither One nor unity. The similarity between Plotinus and Dionysius lies in the similarity of their common language but does not go to the root of their teaching. This distinction has not always been accepted in the West, and Altaner, in his influential handbook of Patrology, describes Dionysius as thoroughly influenced by neoplatonism, the fundamental ideas of which he tried to integrate with Christian doctrine.[6]

It must be kept in mind that unknowability does not mean agnosticism or refusal to seek God. The negative way is a path searching for union, not knowledge. It is not an abstract system, working through concepts, but a form of prayer which raises the subject to that Reality which passes all understanding. In such contemplation the truths of revelation are not suppressed but there is a change of heart, a purification, that enables the seeker to reach out to God Himself.[7]

The Divine Darkness

The origins of Dionysius' mystical theology are found in the teaching of Philo of Alexandria and St. Gregory of Nyssa. Both the latter saw the Book of Exodus as an allegory of spiritual growth. In his *Life of Moses* Gregory first develops the theme of darkness as a metaphor for sin (the Johannine darkness that opposes the Light which has come into the world) but after Moses has left the darkness of sin and begun to climb the mountain he must again enter darkness: this time the divine darkness which surrounds the Godhead. The same distinction is clearly made in Gregory's *Commentary on the Song of Songs:*

> Our initial withdrawal from wrong and erroneous ideas of God is a transition from darkness to light. Next comes a closer awareness of hidden things, and by this the soul is guided through sense phenomena to the world of the invisible. And this awareness is a kind of cloud, which overshadows all appearances, and slowly guides and accustoms the soul to look towards what is hidden. Next the soul makes progress through all these stages and goes on higher, and

16

as she leaves behind all that human nature can attain, she enters within the secret chamber of the divine knowledge, and here she is cut off on all sides by the divine darkness. Now she leaves outside all that can be grasped by sense or by reason, and the only thing left for her contemplation is the invisible and the incomprehensible.[8]

The point is repeated shortly afterwards in a poetical fashion redolent of St. John of the Cross: "The Bride is surrounded with the divine night in which the Bridegroom comes near without showing Himself . . . but by giving the soul a certain sense of His presence while fleeing from clear knowledge."[9]

Like Moses, the Christian seeking union with God must leave behind all surface appearances, intellectual as well as those perceived by the senses, and keep going deeper until by the help of the Holy Spirit he penetrates the invisible. "The true vision and the true knowledge of what we seek consists precisely in not seeing, in an awareness that our goal transcends all knowledge and is everywhere cut off from us by the darkness of incomprehensibility."[10]

The spiritual ascent is a dynamic one. It is always in process. The contemplative life never stops growing towards what is better and never places any limit on perfection. It is impossible for love of the infinite God ever to be sated: "The soul that looks up towards God and conceives that good desire for His eternal beauty, constantly experiences an ever new yearning for that which lies ahead and her desire is never given its full satisfaction."[11]

Paradoxically, though man's desire for God is insatiable, through purification and complete concentration he achieves a state of inner tranquillity (*hesychia*). "Hesychasm" is one of the major strands of Orthodox piety. This form of prayer is a medieval flowering of the negative tradition that is closely associated with control of the physical faculties. In the thirteenth century hesychast monks described their elaborate system of breath control, with the chin resting on the breast and the eyes concentrating on the navel while the practitioner ceaselessly repeated the Jesus Prayer. In this fashion the monk prepared himself for absolute quietude. St. John Climacus, one of the early writers of the tradition, had said, "Let the remembrance of Jesus be present with each breath, and then you will know the value of hesychasm."

Hesychasm was often criticised in the West and during the first half of the fourteenth century Barlaam the Calabrian denounced it violently as an aberration. The great defender of the system and the outstanding Orthodox theologian of the middle ages was Gregory Palamas, Archbishop of Thessalonica from 1347 to 1359. Gregory was born into a family of imperial court dignitaries and having completed his philosophical and theological studies he became a monk on Mount Athos, the centre of hesychasm. After living there for nearly twenty-five years he was drawn into the defence of hesychasm and the last twelve years of his life were spent between Constantinople, where he attended a number of councils and synods, and his archiepiscopal see.

The Divine Light

The starting point of Gregory's mystical theology is the duality of approaches outlined by Dionysius.[12] Unlike his predecessor in the West, St. Thomas Aquinas, Palamas accepts no synthesis of the positive and negative ways. There is a definite antinomy between them and, claimed Gregory, it discloses to us a mysterious distinction in the very being of God: the contrast between the divine essence and the divine energies. This distinction is an effort to resolve the dilemma at the heart of negative theology, the fact that God is both incommunicable and yet the object of mystical union.

It is an accepted belief of Christian faith that we are partakers of the divine nature (2 Peter 1:4) but, adds Gregory, "the divine nature must be said to be at the same time both exclusive of, and, in some sense, open to participation. We attain to participation in the divine nature, and yet at the same time it remains totally inaccessible. We need to affirm both at the same time and to preserve the antinomy as a criterion of right devotion."[13] According to Gregory, therefore, we cannot be united to the essence of God because to be so would mean we were God by nature. His solution to the problem is the notion of the divine energies. These energies are not effects exterior to the divine being such as the material creation but rather are uncreated forces proper to God's essence through which He manifests and communicates Himself. "To say that the divine nature is communicable not in itself but through its energy, is to remain within the bounds of right devotion."

The uncreated energies are the overflowing of the essence and are only inferior to it in the way in which the Son or Holy Spirit can be said to be inferior to the Father, source of divine life within the Trinity. While God remains unknowable in His being, He gives Himself totally in His energies. The fullness of knowledge given to the blessed in heaven is in no way reduced because they are only able to know God through His energies. Insofar as they are given to us to accomplish the work of our sanctification the energies are called grace.

Another and indeed preferred way of speaking of the energies is that of divine light. "God is called light not according to His essence, but according to His energy." Gregory's is very much a theology of light and the Transfiguration of Our Lord had a central place in his thought. He saw the light which surrounded Jesus on Mount Tabor as the eternal, infinite light of God existing outside time and space. Because of His union with the divine nature Christ was filled with this light from the first moment of His birth. While generally it remained invisible to others, at the moment of the Transfiguration a change was

effected in the apostles so that they could contemplate for a moment their Master as He really was:
"The light of the Lord's Transfiguration had no
beginning and no end, it remained uncircumscribed
and imperceptible to the senses, although it was con-
templated by corporeal eyes. By a transmutation of
their senses the disciples of the Lord passed from the
flesh to the Spirit."[14]

The goal of all human contemplation is an experience of the divine light. Symeon the New
Theologian refused the name of Christian to those
who had not experienced this light and according to
Lossky the theology of Light is fundamental to Orthodox spirituality. "One can be completely ignorant
of Gregory Palamas, of his role in the doctrinal
history of the Church of the East; but one can never
understand Eastern spirituality if one makes an
abstraction of its theological basis, which finds its
definitive expression in the great archbishop of
Thessalonica."[15]

Gregory's distinction between God's essence and
His energy is commonly held by modern Orthodox
theologians as the way of defining mystical union
with God and the survey of Palamite writing published in 1972 indicates the continuing impact of this
later Father of the Oriental Church.[16] He is the
eastern Doctor of Divine Grace and his word gives
theological expression to the foundations of Orthodox spirituality.

The Place
of
Jesus Christ

The spirituality of the Western Church lays great stress on the humanity of Jesus. While its first thousand years were dominated by a concern for Christ's divinity, the second millennium has emphasised His humanity. This is not to say, of course, that on January 1st, 1001 a great change was inaugurated, but we do find from the beginning of the middle ages a swing from the Christological themes that had preoccupied early Christianity to a more intense awareness of the events of Our Lord's life, especially His birth and passion. This development climaxed with Francis of Assisi, the saint of the stigmata and the first to construct a crib celebrating the Christmas story.

In the Eastern Church it is not quite so. Orthodox spirituality, while it stresses the Incarnation as the foundation of Christian faith, does not have our forms of devotion to the humanity of Jesus. It is rather through the veneration of icons, which in a very real way brings Christ among us, that the Orthodox behold the life of Jesus. Since the seventh century icons have depicted Jesus in His humanity (instead of in the form of a Lamb) and the defence of these images was based on the theology of the Incarnation which had deepened during the previous centuries.

The Incarnation of the Word still remains the starting point of eastern Christology. Their approach stresses that it is the divine Son who has come among us and so in that sense it is unashamedly "high." There is no quest for the historical Jesus among the Orthodox and to see the Gospels as only records of the deeds of Jesus the Man is foreign to them. Even the two conflicting schools of the fourth and fifth centuries, Antioch and Alexandria, took the divine Word as their point of departure. There is no separation in the East between who Jesus *was* and what He *did* for the two are seen as intimately linked together. What He achieved depended on who He was: "The debates about the identity of Jesus Christ, which lasted for centuries of early Christian history, were neither abstract nor purely academic. For both the words and the acts of Jesus have a different validity and different significance if they proceed from a mere man, or from the second person of the divine Trinity, if they represent a simple episode of human history, or should be seen and believed as unique words and acts of the Lord of history himself. It also makes a tremendous difference for the understanding of who God himself is, whether one sees him as an impassible ruler of a world where good and evil, joy and suffering, life and death are in constant opposition, or whether, on the contrary, one believes that he assumed the human condition, made it his own, and was crucified as a criminal under Pontius Pilate, to rise on the third day, thus vanquishing evil and death."[1]

The First Ecumenical Councils

Oriental spirituality is dominated by the traditions of the early centuries, the Christological centuries, and the classical commentaries and expositions of the Greek Fathers of the Church. The first councils and the controversies surrounding them encompass the very substance of eastern piety. "The theological doctrines which have been elaborated in the course of these struggles can be treated in the most direct relation to the vital end — that of union with God — to the attainment of which they are subservient. Thus they appear as the foundations of Christian spirituality."[2]

The Council of Nicea (325 A.D.) remains the touchstone of Orthodox devotion to Christ. The definition that Jesus is of the same nature as the Father is the supreme expression of classical Christology and, in practical terms, it defends the possibility of our union with God. *Theosis*, deification, is the ultimate end of man according to the Greek Fathers. God became man so that men could become gods. The Arians, on the contrary, accepted Jesus merely as the most worthy of God's creatures and denied that He was eternal, that He was divine. The Church affirmed the dogma of the consubstantial Son for it is through the Word, that we are united to the Godhead: if the Word has not the same nature as the Father, if He is not truly divine, our deification is impossible.

The great defender of the Nicene creed, St. Athanasius, explained the term "consubstantial" as simply meaning that whatever attributes the Father receives can also be given to the Son, except the name "Father," and from that point of view the definition is not limited to its own cultural context but remains true for all times and places. It is certainly held as valid in the Orthodox Church today.

It was the same concern to uphold the possibility of union with God through Jesus Christ that led to the condemnation of Nestorius at the Council of Ephesus in 431 A.D. The central issue now was the personal unity of Jesus Christ. The followers of Nestorius seemed to be introducing a wall of partition whereby, in the person of Jesus, they would have separated God from man. To put it in crude terms, the Nestorian view spoke of two persons in Jesus Christ, the divine (subject of the divine actions) and the human (subject of the human actions).

The outstanding defender of the Orthodox faith this time and one who has left an enduring mark on the Eastern Church was Cyril of Alexandria. It was not only through his ideas but also through his theological method that Cyril influenced matters. He is in fact the chief exponent among the Greek

Fathers of what was to become their favourite procedure. He consciously and purposely extended the well established practice of drawing arguments from the Bible to include also proofs from the Fathers. While he did not invent the method, nobody before him had used it with such skill and it is largely due to him that patristic testimony stands alongside Sacred Scripture as the authority in all matters of debate: "We shall succeed in rightly expounding the doctrine of faith to those who are seeking the truth if, betaking ourselves to the statements of the Fathers, we are careful to esteem them highly and putting our own selves to test as to whether we are in the faith, as it is written (2 Corinthians 13:5), thoroughly conform our own beliefs to their sound and unexceptional doctrines."

The Council of Ephesus shared Cyril's view that the Holy Fathers spoke under the guidance of the Spirit and adopted the patristic argument in its deliberations. Since then it has become the established practice of all eastern theologians, though it is also standard in the West.

In his teaching Cyril of Alexandria insisted on the unity of the person Jesus Christ (the hypostatic union). There is one person, Jesus Christ, who is both God and man. To reject this unity is to conclude that there are two sons. "We do not affirm that the nature of the Word underwent a change and became flesh, or that it was transformed into a whole or perfect man consisting of soul and body; but we say that the Word took flesh making it His own, thus becoming man and was called the Son of Man, yet not of mere will or favour, nor again by the simple taking to Himself of a person (i.e. of a human person to His divine person), and that while the natures which were brought together into this true unity were diverse there was of both one Christ and one Son; not as though the diverseness of the natures were done away by this union, but rather the Godhead and Manhood completed for us the one Lord and Christ and Son by their inutterable and unspeakable concurrence and unity."[3]

According to a modern scholar the root of Nestorius' heresy was a failure to grasp the traditional doctrine of the "exchange of attributes."[4] This term was adopted by the Greek Fathers to define more closely the interchange of divine and human qualities pertaining to Jesus Christ as the result of the Incarnation. Because Jesus is a single person subsisting in a divine and human nature we can attribute to Him not only these two natures but also the qualities inherent in each nature since they all belong to one and the same person. The "exchange of attributes" is vividly illustrated in the striking declaration of the eastern monks: "One of the Trinity was crucified for us" and in his twelfth anathema against Nestorius, Cyril of Alexandria defended the formula that "the Word suffered in the flesh."

As a direct result of the interchange of attributes Mary can truly be called the Mother of God (*Theotokos*), her most privileged title among the Orthodox. In a later reflection on this name St. John Damascene stated that it "summarises all the mystery of the economy (of salvation), for if the mother is *Theotokos*, it is because her Son is surely God and surely man."[5] Eastern piety honours the Blessed Virgin because she alone was found worthy to bear the Word made flesh. Her cooperation was essential. "The incarnation," explained the fourteenth century Byzantine theologian Nicholas Cabasilas, "was not only the work of the Father, by His power and by His spirit, but it was also the work of the will and faith of the Virgin. Without the consent of the immaculate, without the agreement of her faith, the plan was as unrealisable as it would have been without the intervention of the three divine Persons themselves. It was only after having instructed her and persuaded her that God took her for His Mother and borrowed from her the flesh, that she so greatly wished to lend Him. Just as He became incarnate voluntarily, so He wished that His Mother should bear Him freely and with her full consent."[6]

The Council of Chalcedon (451) was the next major step along the path of Christian dogma. This ecumenical gathering was to be the centre of a theological dispute which caused the most serious defection from unity that the Church had so far experienced and it effected a split within eastern Christianity which remains to the present day. The origins of the trouble lay in an exaggerated emphasis on the divine nature of Jesus Christ. Abbot Eutyches of Alexandria so stressed the divine aspect of Christ that he denied, in practice, that He was fully human: Jesus had not the same nature as other men. His humanity was "absorbed" by the divinity, like melting wax by flame.

In response Chalcedon drew up its definition:

"Following then the holy Fathers, we all with one voice teach that it should be confessed that our Lord Jesus Christ is one and the same Son, the Same perfect in Godhead, the Same perfect in manhood, truly God and truly man, the Same (consisting) of a rational soul and a body; consubstantial with the Father as to his Godhead, and the same consubstantial with us as to his manhood; in all things like us, sin only excepted; begotten of the Father before ages as to his Godhead, and in the last days, the Same, for us and for our salvation, of Mary the Virgin Theotokos as to his manhood."

The council went on to describe the union of the divine and human natures in Christ by four negative adverbs: without confusion, without change, without division, without separation. Far from claiming to have resolved the mystery of the Incarnation, therefore, the Fathers tried to maintain the element of mystery amid the intricacies and subtleties into which they had been plunged.

That Chalcedon was a beginning rather than an end is well illustrated by Meyendorff's erudite study of the theological movements of the succeeding centuries.[7] Yet the great outline had been given and the basic foundations laid. The early councils remained the ultimate guarantee of the Orthodox position. Even the iconoclast party of 754, led by the emperor Constantine V, claimed the support of Chalcedon in its attempt to suppress the veneration of statues and icons. More about that later.

One final name worth mentioning is that of St. John Damascene (749), reckoned to be the last of the

Greek Fathers, because his theological synthesis was to be the manual of the Byzantine middle ages. He based his Christology on Chalcedon though he took into account the developments of the sixth and seventh centuries. John underlined the divine aspect of Jesus Christ. Thus while the two natures of Jesus are distinct and unmixed, the divine permeates the flesh of Christ since His humanity is diffused by the uncreated energies from the moment of the Incarnation. As iron penetrated by fire becomes fire while still remaining iron, each act of Jesus involves two distinct operations because in conformity to both his human and divine natures.

The Orthodox Church never considers the humanity of Christ apart from His Godhead. This is borne out by the solemn festivals of the Baptism of Jesus and the Transfiguration which serve as a key to understanding the place of Jesus' humanity in the eastern tradition. In both celebrations it is the Trinity that is honoured: the voice of the Father is heard and the Holy Spirit is seen either in the form of a dove or as the luminous cloud which covered the apostles. This royal aspect of Christ "is characteristic of Orthodox spirituality in every epoch and in every country. Even the Passion, the death on the cross, and the laying in the tomb become triumphant acts by which the Divine Majesty of Christ illuminates the images of the fall and abandonment whilst accomplishing the mystery of our salvation."[8]

Prayer to Christ in the Liturgy

The Arian struggle had a profound effect on the early Church, especially in the East. One of the most obvious results of the conflict was the greater place given to Jesus in liturgical prayer. This becomes evident when we consider the developments which took place at the time.

It is certainly true that even in the New Testament we find prayers directed to Christ. He was not only a great teacher of prayer but according to St. John's Gospel He is the determining factor of good prayer. Indeed, He Himself answers our prayers: "If you ask me anything in my name, I will do it." (John 14:14) Commitment to the person of Jesus and total love (Matthew 10:32) are asked of the disciples and after the Resurrection they bow down to Him in worship. At the name of Jesus every knee should bow, wrote St. Paul in Philippians 2:10.

Yet the stress of New Testament teaching is that Jesus Christ is the intermediary of our prayer. He is the one standing between God and man who has come not to be served but to serve and give life as a ransom for many. He emptied Himself of His privileges so that He could bring us to the Father. Christians are those who call upon the name of Jesus and following the example of St. Paul they are exhorted "to do everything in the name of the Lord Jesus, giving thanks to God the Father through him." (Colossians 3:17) In the same way St. Peter calls upon the faithful to use the gifts they have received "in order that in everything God may be glorified through Jesus Christ." (1 Peter 4:11)

The phrase "through him" was gradually introduced into prayer and became customary in public worship. The faithful, through their Amen, proclaimed their union with the prayers offered in the name of Christ the Saviour. The theme of mediation is central to the Letter to the Hebrews: Jesus is our Great High Priest who sits at the right hand of the Father continuously interceding for us. The same notion underlines the description of Jesus as a Paraclete (1 John 2:1). Like the Holy Spirit He is our advocate or counsellor, the one who pleads our case in the court of heaven.

The early liturgy of both East and West preserves the basic thrust of New Testament formulae. Prayer is addressed through Christ the Lord to the Father. A collection of prayers and ceremonies known as *The Apostolic Tradition* gives a clear insight into the liturgical structure traditional by the end of the third century. Jesus is "the child of God" and the book always puts Him in an intermediary position with expressions such as "through thy Christ," "through Jesus Christ our Hope." This western approach is summed up in Canon 21 of the Council of Hippo (393 A.D.) which decreed that at the altar "prayers must always be directed to the Father."

The eastern liturgies maintained the same orientation. A good example is the *Euchologium* of Bishop Serapion, a manuscript discovered in the Hagian Laura monastery on Mount Athos in 1898. Serapion was bishop of Thmuis from 339 to 362 and his *Euchologium* contains thirty-seven prayers for the celebration of the Eucharist. They are all addressed to God the Father and the conclusions are a praise of the Father through Jesus Christ in the Holy Spirit. Such endings had spread throughout the East by the fourth century and are reflected in the common pre-Nicene doxology: "Glory be to the Father, through the Son, in the Holy Spirit."[9]

The mediation of Christ in the liturgy was seized upon by the Arians as a proof of His subordination to the Father. They eagerly collected all the scriptural texts which spoke of a "humbling" of the Son, e.g. Philippians 2:8. They argued that the Church herself recognises the inferiority of Christ to the Father in her daily prayers. They claimed that the orthodox were being illogical in constantly putting the Father before the Son in the liturgy and credal statements and then condemning the Arians for doing the same in their theology.

Replying to the Arians, the Fathers fell back on the distinction between *theology* and *economy*. Prayer is a matter which pertains to the created order: it is made when God becomes present in the history of salvation (economy). As man Jesus fulfills His priestly role in heaven but this must not be confused with His divine relationship of equality with the Father (theology). Cyril of Alexandria commented on John 16:23: "Along with the Father, he bestows good things on the saints . . . but in that he is named Mediator and High Priest and Advocate he offers the prayer to the Father for us. For he is the source of confidence of us all before the Father."[10]

The Arians refused to accept these distinctions and the liturgical formulae became slogans for their teaching. In two important ones of the East, Antioch and Cappadocia, the dispute centred on the doxologies and the Orthodox began to abandon the traditional prayer endings (which were recited by the Arians with great emphasis at the appropriate places) in favour of newer forms giving no possibility of misrepresentation. In place of the customary pre-Nicene doxology they introduced the form "glory be to the Father, to the Son and to the Holy Spirit" and the two doxologies became the catchwords of the opposing parties. It is said that Bishop Leontius of Antioch (344-358), who had Arian sympathies but wanted to retain the good will of the Catholics always recited the doxology in silence so that even those standing beside him could only hear the final words "for ever and ever. Amen."

The Bishop of Cappadocia, St. Basil the Great, was made of sterner stuff. In fact he was the leader of the Orthodox party. Amid a storm of protest from the Arians he introduced a new doxology: "Glory be to the Father *with* the Son *together* with the Holy Spirit." It was to justify the innovation, denounced by his opponents as alien to the liturgical traditions, that Basil composed his classical work *On the Holy Spirit*.

Basil made a thorough examination of the different doxologies. It is true, as the Arians never failed to point out, that the New Testament often speaks of creation and redemption coming into being through Christ. But, argued Basil, there is nothing fixed or irrevocable in the use of these prepositions and they certainly do not indicate an order of precedence among the divine persons. As far as rank is concerned (theology), the same honour is due to the Father, the Son and the Holy Spirit. In prayer (the order of economy), we acknowledge that all good things have come to us from God through Jesus and in Him. Basil's new formula *with* corresponds to adoration; the phrase *through him* belongs to thanksgiving. Both are proper and justified. Basil therefore accepted the traditional form but because of Arian misinterpretation did not value it highly.

From now on we find more direct invocation of Jesus Christ in the eastern liturgies. One of the most ancient was the popular "Kyrie eleison" first attested in *The Apostolic Constitutions* of the fourth century and which eventually found its way even into the Roman canon! This invocation, coming as it does before the eucharistic prayer, is, of course, a secondary element of the liturgy yet it is a good indication of the direction taken as a result of the Arian controversy. In the liturgy of St. James we find a short litany in the heart of the canon similar to our first proclamation: "Christ has died, Christ is risen, Christ will come again."

After the fourth century it could be said in general that prayer through Christ went into decline.

There was a diminishing importance given to the place of Jesus as the Great High Priest constantly interceding for His Body, the Church. Instead there was a tendency in the West during the middle ages to contemplate His passion and death and in the East to put a stronger emphasis on His divinity.

The Jesus Prayer

From the beginning of the Church Christians were defined as those who "call upon the name of Jesus" (Acts 9:14) and it was this prayer which distinguished them from the Jews. In the West the Holy Name has always been honoured, especially in medieval times, and it was, for example, one of the few feasts which survived the drastic pruning of the Reformation in England.

The Jesus prayer ("Lord Jesus Christ, Son of God, be merciful to me, a sinner") is greatly recommended by the Orthodox as the simplest and most effective aid to contemplation. Its origins can be traced back to the Fathers of the Desert. Literally interpreting St. Paul's injunction in 1 Thessalonians 5:17, these monks dedicated themselves to God by continuous prayer. They resolved, to some extent, the psychological difficulty of keeping their minds fixed on God by the practice of aspirations and they preferred such short ejaculations to lengthy, formal meditation. Naturally, they did not consider the verbal repetition of words as salutary in itself: it had to be accompanied by a purification of the heart. This purification

demanded not only observance of the command-
ments and virtuous living but also a constant guard
over the imagination and the senses. The monks
sought to control their wayward and wandering
thoughts and they believed that the most efficacious
remedy to distraction was a continual practice of
ejaculatory prayer. At the beginning there was no
fixed form to the invocations.

From about the fifth century onwards we find a
privileged place being given to the Holy Name. The
following text (wrongly attributed to St. John
Chrysostom) reflects the flowering of the movement
and the false authorship was to give the passage a
stamp of orthodoxy that guaranteed its acceptance
by succeeding generations:

"I implore you, brethren, never to abandon
the rule of prayer or neglect it. Eating and drink-
ing, at home or on a journey, or whatever else he
does, a monk should constantly call: 'Lord, Jesus
Christ, Son of God, have mercy on me.' This re-
membering of the name of our Lord Jesus Christ
should incite him to battle with the enemy. By
this remembrance a soul forcing itself to this practice can discover everything which is within, both
good and bad. First it will see within, in the heart,
what is bad, and later — what is good. . . . The
name of our Lord Jesus Christ, descending into
the depths of the heart will subdue the serpent
holding sway over the pastures of the heart and
will save our soul and bring it to life. Thus abide
constantly with the name of our Lord Jesus
Christ, so that the heart swallows the Lord and
the Lord the heart and the two become one. But

this work is not done in one or two days; it needs many years and a long time. For great and prolonged labour is needed to cast out the foe so that Christ dwells in us."[11]

The monastic communities of Mount Athos founded at the beginning of the eleventh century became the centre of Orthodox spirituality and witnessed a great resurgence during the second half of the thirteenth century. As was mentioned in the previous chapter the invocation of the Holy Name was now accompanied by a complex technique of breath control that was to give hesychast prayer its own definitive expression. Some authors see here an influence on Byzantine spirituality from Muslim asceticism and perhaps the ultimate sources lie in the Far East, especially Hindu Yoga and Zen Buddhism.

Gregory of Sinai (†1346), one of the founders of hesychasm on Mount Athos, is our most reliable guide for details of the movement's prayer forms. According to Gregory the potential gift of the Holy Spirit (the energy of the Holy Spirit) received sacramentally at baptism can be the object of personal experience. The quickest way to achieve this is by the methodical use of the Jesus prayer and he gives concrete details as to how to proceed with the matter. Proper moral dispositions (a pure conscience and detachment from passions) are of course presupposed and the external conditions include the right choice of place (a quiet darkened cell is preferred), correct physical posture (a bent sitting position) and control of the breathing. In this way one is meant to explore his "heart," that is to say, one gathers together the thoughts and imaginations which so easily lead to distraction and concentrates them on the core of one's being. Yet in this state of complete recollection a person is not totally passive because there must be a frequent repetition of the Jesus prayer. To avoid monotony Gregory advises his reader to change the words of the prayer and to alternate between verbal and mental recitation. Above all, it is essential to remain tranquil throughout the exercise.

Hesychasm was strongly criticised during the fourteenth century. At the time of the dispute Gregory Palamas was a monk on Mount Athos and he eventually became the chief defender of the monks. He recognized that certain techniques were exaggerated, an abuse he attributed to the ignorance of some of his predecessors, and he conceded that in physical matters the Spirit has given us no clear revelation. The important point, he argued, is to see that the body is not a hindrance but in fact can help the one who is praying and so transformed by the Holy Spirit it becomes "a house of God."[12]

Modern commentators on the Jesus prayer carefully distinguish it from the bodily postures that have accompanied it. Orthodox Bishop Anthony Bloom states: "Numerous writers have mentioned the physical aspects of the prayer, the breathing exercises, the attention which is paid to the beating of the heart and a number of other minor features. The Philokalia is full of detailed instructions about the prayer of the heart, even with reference to the Sufi technique. Ancient and modern Fathers have dealt with the subject, always coming to the same conclusion: never to attempt the physical exercises without strict guidance by a spiritual father."

What is of general use, the bishop concludes, is the actual praying, the repetition of the words, without any physical endeavour. More than any other prayer, he writes, the Jesus prayer aims at bringing us to stand in God's presence with no other thought but the miracle of our standing there and God with us, because in the use of the Jesus prayer there is nothing and no one except God and us.[13]

The Holy Spirit

Western spirituality, both Catholic and Protestant, has traditionally put Jesus Christ at the centre of prayer and devotion. So strong has been this preoccupation that we are accused by the Orthodox of forgetting the Holy Spirit. During the Second Vatican Council, for example, the eastern theologians present as observers felt it necessary to remind the bishops preparing the Constitution on the Church to focus more sharply on the role of the Holy Spirit.

In the East the Spirit has a position similar to what we give to Jesus. The doctrine of the Holy Spirit (Pneumatology) informs every aspect of devotion, for as a modern writer comments: "To speak of orthodox pneumatology does not mean exposing a doctrine of the Holy Spirit. The Holy Spirit cannot become a formula, a dogma apart. Pneumatology is the heart of Christian theology, it touches all aspects of faith in Christ. It is a commentary on the acts of the revealed triune God, the life of the Church, and of the man who prays and is regenerated. Orthodox pneumatology does not allow the doctrine of the Holy Spirit to become a separate chapter of dogmatic theology." If the first eight centuries of Orthodoxy were concerned with Christology, from the ninth onwards we find a stress on the Holy Spirit which culminated in the synods of Constantinople during the fourteenth century.[1]

In this area of faith too it is the teaching of the Greek Fathers that is still the major influence. According to them the Church is built on the two-fold mission of the Son and the Holy Spirit. They used the word "economy" to describe the relationship of each divine person to history: the work of Jesus and of the Spirit complement one another and these two "economies" are the foundations of the Church. Christ is the Head of the Church, His Body, and the Holy Spirit animates and gives it life. Both are intimately linked together in the saving plan of the Father. St. Gregory of Nyssa succinctly described this unity of purpose and individual manifestation of the three persons: "One does not think of the Father without the Son, one does not conceive of the Son without the Holy Spirit. For it is impossible to attain to the Father except by being raised by the Son, and it is impossible to call Jesus Lord save in the Holy Spirit."[2]

Gregory of Nyssa, together with Basil and Gregory Nazianzen, form the trio known as the Great Cappadocians (from their place of origin) who defended the doctrine of the Holy Spirit in the fourth century and gave Orthodox theology its formal trinitarian structure. Gregory Nazianzen explained the successive revelations of the Father, Son and Spirit as follows: "The Old Testament manifested the

Father plainly, the Son obscurely. The New Testament revealed the Son and hinted at the divinity of the Holy Spirit. Today the Spirit dwells among us and makes Himself more clearly known. For it was not safe, when the Godhead of the Father was not yet acknowledged, plainly to proclaim the Son; nor when that of the Son was not yet received to burden us further (if I may use so bold an expression) with the Holy Spirit ... but rather that by gradual additions, and, as David says, goings up and advances and progress from glory to glory, the light of the Trinity might shine upon the more illuminated."[3]

St. Basil's work on the Holy Spirit, together with Athanasius' *Letters to Serapion*, remained the standard works of pneumatology and during the Byzantine middle ages, apart from the matter of the *Filioque*, there was little further development. What was stressed later was the experience of the Spirit in hymns, sacramental theology and spiritual literature.[4]

The Procession of the Holy Spirit

The relationship of the Holy Spirit to the Son is one of the disputed points of the ecumenical dialogue between East and West. Though it may seem an abstract point to us the question has an important bearing on the spirituality of the Orthodox Church.

The Greeks reject the credal statement that the Spirit proceeds from the Father "and from the Son" (*Filioque*) on historical and dogmatic grounds. First of all, they consider it a later addition to the symbol of faith drawn up at the councils of Nicea and Constantinople and in support they quote Cyril of Alexandria who declared that to omit or add anything to that creed of the universal Church would be equivalent to contradicting the Holy Spirit. Thus when French monks in Jerusalem chanted the *Filioque* during the Credo at the beginning of the ninth century they were accused of heresy by the Greeks. Even the Roman Popes were hesitant about making the addition until finally Benedict VIII accepted the Germanic rite of 1014 and the *Filioque* was sung in St. Peter's.

The central reason for the Orthodox rejection of the phrase is neither historical nor (as has often been suggested) political. It results from a belief in the unique role of the Father as author of life within the Trinity (the "monarchy" of the Father). This was expressed in lapidary fashion by St. Athanasius: "There is only one principal, not two, of divinity. This principal is God, from whom comes the Word." The controversy over the *Filioque*, therefore, has its roots in the eastern understanding of the Trinity and of God's interpersonal life with the Son and the Holy Spirit.

As was said in chapter one, Greek theologians approach the mystery of the Trinity with the three persons as their starting point whereas in the West, the unity of the divine nature is considered first. The orientals emphasise that the Father, not the nature, gives life to the other two persons. According to Gregory of Nyssa, for example, the Father alone is the principle of union within the Godhead and Gregory Naziazen insisted that "The Son possesses everything the Father has except the ability to be cause."[5]

In accordance with their theological method the eastern Fathers concluded that the origin of the Holy Spirit is ineffable and they did not try to define the matter too closely. To quote Gregory Nazianzen again: "The Holy Spirit is truly Spirit, coming forth from the Father indeed, but not after the manner of the Son, for it is not by generation but by procession since I must coin a word for the sake of clearness." In what precisely this "procession" consisted Gregory admitted he could not explain. Basil merely said that the Spirit "comes forth as a breath from the mouth of the Father" in a manner unutterable. Gregory of Nyssa saw a difference in the fact that the Holy Spirit proceeds from the

51

Father and "receives" from the Son, but the intimate nature of the union baffled him also.

This tradition has been maintained by modern Orthodox scholars, though some of them show a greater broadness of opinion on the matter than others. At the end of the last century Bolotov, a Russian historian of dogma who had been engaged with Old Catholics in a number of ecumenical debates, concluded after a careful analysis of the patristic texts that the *Filioque* does not constitute an insurmountable obstacle to reunion as long as it is not claimed that the Son is a *cause* of the Spirit's personhood. If this is granted the *Filioque* can be seen as complementary to the Orthodox position that the Holy Spirit comes from the Father "through the Son" *(dia Uiou)*. The two formulae, each in its own way, faithfully describe the procession of the Holy Spirit.

Lossky, however, was not happy with the above conclusion which, he hinted, was a devaluation rather than a revaluation of the tradition. Yet even he admitted the possibility of an Orthodox interpretation of the *Filioque*.[6] A more recent writer, Paul Evdokimov, follows up the lines opened by Bolotov and though himself rejecting any notion of causality accepts the Son's role in the procession of the Holy Spirit from the Father as a necessary condition. In other words, the Spirit cannot be seen in isolation from the other persons just as indeed the Godhead of the Father and the generation of the Son are in their turn also actions of the whole Trinity. What Evdokimov underlines, and it seems to be the crux of the matter, is that rejection or affirmation of the

Filioque has not made the slightest difference to the adoration given to the Spirit both in East and West. This lack of liturgical or theological consequence indicates that whatever the actual solution to the division may be, neither formula can be substantially opposed to the other.[7]

The Economy of the Holy Spirit

Faithful to the patristic example, Orthodox piety is rooted in contemplation of the Blessed Trinity. In its prayer life it strives to avoid exclusive concentrations on either the Son or the Holy Spirit so that it can maintain a proper harmony in its adoration of the three persons. Even the feast of Pentecost is primarily a trinitarian celebration, the Monday following being devoted to the Holy Spirit. The Church is the earthly reflection of the divine community and its purpose is to glorify the Father, the Son and the Holy Spirit. The baptised are given a share in the divine nature and God is asked, in a prayer for those about to be confirmed, to seal the faithful with the immaculate chrism so that they will carry Christ in their hearts and become a trinitarian dwelling-house.

The Church, built on the two-fold economy of the Son and the Spirit, is filled with the fullness of grace. As St. Irenaeus wrote: "Where the Church is, there is the Spirit; where the Spirit is, there is the Church." The two missions are intimately linked together, even though they remain proper to the two persons. Pentecost is neither a replacement of nor subordinate to the incarnation, but rather its fruit and sequel. Having perfected His work in Jesus Christ the Holy Spirit can now be poured out on all mankind. Unlike the birth of Jesus, however, the Spirit does not become incarnate: He remains hidden even after Pentecost. As a result Orthodox piety calls on the Spirit with the paradoxical invocations of the Byzantine mystic Symeon the New Theologian:

> Come, true light; come, eternal life; come, hidden mystery; come, treasure without name; come, unutterable thing; come, unknowable person; come, O powerful one, who fulfillest, transformest and changest all things by thy will alone; come, invisible one, wholly intangible and impalpable. Come, thou who restest always immovable and who, at all times, movest thyself and comest toward us who lie in hell. Thou standest higher than the heavens. Thy name so greatly and constantly proclaimed, none is able to say what it is. None can know who thou art, of what kind or species, for that is impossible. Come, garland never withered; come thou whom my wretched soul has loved and whom it loves! Come alone to me alone. Come, thou who hast separated me from all and hast made me lonely in this world and who thyself are become desire in me, who hast willed that I should desire thee, thou, absolutely inaccessible. Come, breath and my own life, consolation of my lowly heart."[8]

The Word and the Spirit are the two hands of the Father and it is through the Eucharist and Pentecost that the Church comes into being. Pentecost is the second act of the Father: first He sent the Son and now He sends the Holy Spirit. Jesus has returned to the Father so that the second Paraclete can come to complete His work and console the disciples after His departure. Pentecost is the climax of the trinitarian work of salvation: "The Word has assumed flesh so that we could receive the Spirit. God has become flesh so that man could become a spirit." (St. Athanasius)

Unlike the western Church, Orthodoxy does not make a clearcut distinction between created and uncreated grace. For the East grace usually signifies the abundance of the divine nature, insofar as it is poured out on the world. The divine nature is given to man through the uncreated energies. The Holy Spirit is the source of these gifts and while remaining mysterious and unrevealed he is given all the titles given to grace: "He is called the Spirit of God, the Spirit of Christ, the Mind of Christ, the Spirit of Adoption, of Truth, of Liberty, the Creator-Spirit, who by baptism and by resurrection creates anew." (Gregory Nazianzen)

Baptism and confirmation are administered together in the oriental rite and through the sacrament of holy chrism the Spirit is considered to descend invisibly on the newly-baptised just as He descended upon the apostles with tongues of fire. The Eastern Church has been spared the difficulty experienced in Latin theology since the fifth century (when the two sacraments began to be conferred separately) of explaining what exactly confirmation adds to baptism. The Spirit is communicated in both sacraments and because of the intimate connection between them the gift of the Spirit is often spoken of as baptismal grace.

For this reason Seraphim of Sarov could write of Pentecost: "This enkindled breath which we faithful Christians all receive in the sacrament of holy baptism is sealed with the sacred seals of holy chrism affixed to the principal parts of our body according to the direction of the Church; for from this moment onwards our body becomes a tabernacle of grace for all eternity."[9]

The Holy Spirit does not come alone when He make His dwelling place within us. The Father and the Son are inseparable from Him and together They bestow on the baptised Their uncreated energies, their glory and Their light. So real is this presence that it cannot remain undisclosed and totally hidden. Basing himself on the Johannine promise that the Spirit will become a spring of life for the believer, Symeon the New Theologian goes so far as to say that anyone who claims to have received the Spirit without any awareness of Him is a blasphemer: "If the spring gushes up within us, the stream which flows from it must of necessity be visible to those who have eyes to see. But if all this happens within us without our having any experience or consciousness of it, then it is certain that we shall not know the eternal life which comes thence, that we shall not see the light of the Holy Spirit; for we shall remain as dead, blind and insensible in the life of eternity as we are in this present life."[10]

The Holy Spirit therefore rests on Christians just as He rested on Jesus, leading them into the kingdom of God, raising up their natures and crying out in their hearts, *Abba*, Father! He prays within them,

57

communicating His own life to them. He is called holy not only because such a title is appropriate: He is all-holy *(panagios)* by His very being. Though each of the three persons is holy, the Spirit is the very holiness of God. Through his indwelling in their hearts, the Spirit shares His holiness with all true believers.

The Invocation of the Holy Spirit in the Liturgy

The prayer life of the Orthodox Church finds its supreme expression in the liturgy. During the centuries of oppression under Turkish rule, when the very existence of the Greek nation was threatened, it was through the liturgical cycle of fast and feast that the ordinary people were able to cling to their religious beliefs. The same is true of the Church in Russia today. "It is because her life is rooted so completely in the liturgy that the Orthodox Church has been able to preserve in all its integrity the faith once delivered to the saints. . . . Even when, as in the U.S.S.R. today, the Church is subject to every imaginable restriction save this bare permission to celebrate the divine mysteries, she can yet contrive to hold fast to her traditions with a tenacity which must often strike the western Christian as little short of miraculous."[11]

The language, hymns and sacraments of cultic life mould and express the essential outlines of eastern spirituality. Liturgical consecration is considered to transform the material elements of bread, wine and oil into an extension of the celestial realms and the splendour of worship is intended to give a foretaste of the glory to be revealed in the kingdom of God. Heaven upon earth is how one commentator sums up the celebration of the oriental rites. Praise issues from the depths of the believer's heart, the inner sanctuary, and is carried by the angels to the heights of the divine presence.

The Orthodox make no division between personal prayer and communal worship: one flows into the other to be enriched and strengthened before returning to its source. As Dom Rousseau observed earlier this century, there can be no question of a liturgical movement in the Eastern Church since her piety has never deviated from her worship. Because of this Gregory Palamas, having lived the traditional silent prayer on Mount Athos, found no difficulty after becoming Archbishop of Thessalonica in preaching salvation through the sacraments to his flock.

The year of grace, the liturgical seasons, centres on the Easter mystery and provides a continual memorial of the events of salvation history. The law of prayer is the law of belief and it is through enacting the mysteries that the Orthodox world has been held together despite continuous persecution by Tartars, Turks and Communists. (One less happy result of the historical struggle is a certain inflexibility of attitude in religious matters, a suspicion of outside influences and an unwillingness to admit that some liturgical reforms may now have become necessary).

The Holy Spirit plays a vital part in the liturgy, the celebration of which provides the most fruitful setting for the bestowal of His gifts. The unanimous tradition of the East, from St. John Chrysostom and

St. Basil in the fourth century to Nicholas Cabasilas in the middle ages and the staretz of our own times, proclaims the presence of the Spirit in the Church now as at the first Pentecost. "Pentecost is a permanent feast," wrote St. John Chrysostom. "If the Spirit were not present the Church would not exist."[12]

The Holy Spirit inspires all prayer, whether personal or liturgical: He invites the Christian to pray, makes his encounter with God possible and transforms him into a temple of the Lord. There is no real difference between the prayer of the heart and liturgical doxology — they both issue from the one source. Issac of Niniveh explains: "When the Spirit takes up his abode in a man the latter cannot cease to pray because the Spirit prays within him. Whether he sleeps or stays awake, prayer is never absent from his soul. From now on he cannot confine his prayers to set times but is moved to pray at all times."[13]

In the Orthodox view there is no access to the Father except through the Son and no access to the Son save by the Holy Spirit. Consequently every act of communion with God is begun with an invocation of the Spirit. On Holy Thursday, for example, the blessing of the oil to be used in confirmation is seen as similar to the consecration of the bread in the eucharist and its key element is the invocation (*epiclesis*) of the Holy Spirit. By such invocation the divine energies come down upon the gifts.

Even though the Latin Church theologians such as St. Augustine and St. Thomas Aquinas held that the consecration of the bread and wine is effected by the power of the Holy Spirit this view is so strongly upheld in the East that it has become a matter of division. The invocation of the Spirit (asking the Father or the Son to send the Holy Spirit to sanctify the gifts on the altar) found in the oriental rites *after* the words of institution is regarded by the Orthodox as the sacred moment in which the bread and wine become the Body and Blood of Christ. They claim the support of Basil the Great and other eminent Fathers and the liturgy of St. John Chrysostom has the following epiclesis after the institution narrative: "We pray and beseech you, send your Holy Spirit on us and upon these gifts placed here and make this bread the precious body of Christ, changing it by the power of your Holy Spirit, and what is in this chalice the precious blood of Christ, changing it by the power of your Holy Spirit."

There are numerous other authorities brought forward by the Orthodox in favour of their position. Evdokimov believes that this dispute is just as significant for the ecumenical dialogue as the question of the *Filioque* and indeed he sees a possibility for agreement on the latter point resulting from a clearer understanding of the epiclesis. He locates the root of the problem in a different (and from our view complementary) understanding of liturgical prayer. According to western theology the celebrant prays at Mass in the person of Christ and so his consecration formula is an invocation (epiclesis) rather than the declaration "This is my Body."[14]

After the transformation of the offerings the Holy Spirit is asked to change the hearts of those who communicate by making them into one Body of

Christ. The term used in Byzantine theology to express this unifying presence of the Spirit in the eucharistic community is *koinonia*. The "oneness" achieved in the liturgy is above all a gift of the Holy Spirit. A number of hymns make the contrast between the confusion of Babel and the harmony realised by the descent of the Spirit: "When the Most High came down and confused the tongues, He divided the nations, but when He distributed the tongues of fire, He called all to unity. Therefore, with one voice, we glorify the all-holy Spirit."[15]

The divine liturgy is the abiding presence of Pentecost and it concludes by sending us forth with the mission given by the Risen Lord when He breathed on the apostles. Therefore in a final hymn we glorify Christ "who has made the fishermen most wise by sending down upon them the Holy Spirit, and through them did draw the world into His net."

In his description of the Holy Spirit's action in the liturgy, Gregory of Sinai (†1346) vividly captures the eastern sense of celebration, clearly underlining both its interior dimension and the demands it makes on practical living: "When the heart has been purified through the presence of the Holy Spirit it becomes a real and everlasting temple where the liturgy is celebrated without hindrance. He who has not yet attained this state may perhaps due to his other virtues be a good stone for the construction of the temple but he cannot be himself the temple of the Holy Spirit nor his high-priest."[16]

The Image of God

Orthodox spirituality is centered on the trinitarian mystery: the Father revealing Himself through the Son in the power of the Holy Spirit. Yet like all spiritualities it presupposes a world-view and a doctrine of man. The key-note of that doctrine is the word *image*. "Let us make man in our image and after our likeness" is the basic scriptural text of eastern anthropology and it is on this sentence from Genesis that the Greek Fathers constructed their theology of creation, grace and prayer.

According to the Bible man's significance stems from the fact that he has been made in the image of God and the priestly authors of Genesis, having portrayed the Creator in terms of free, conscious activity, depict the first couple sharing similar power over the rest of the world. It is precisely because he is capable of self-awareness and self-determination that man reflects the life of God and is capable of entering into a relationship with Him.

The outstanding biblical scholar among the Greek Fathers, Origen, built his whole theology around the concept of "image" and commenting on this Lossky refers to the centrality of the theme in Christian revelation:

"If man is *logikos*, to use here an expression of Origen's, if he is 'in the image' of the Logos, everything which touches the destiny of man — grace, sin, redemption by the Word made man — must also be related to the theology of the image. And we may say the same of the Church, the sacraments, spiritual life, sanctification, and the end of all things. There is not a branch of theological teaching which can be entirely isolated from the problem of the image without danger of severing it from the living stock of Christian tradition."[1]

Christ the Image of God

St. Paul describes Jesus Christ as the image of the invisible God, the first-born of all creation (Colossians 1:15) and the theme was developed by the early Fathers, especially Origen and Gregory of Nyssa. Sharing the same divine nature as His Father, though personally distinct from Him, the Son is best described as the Father's natural substantial image: the Logos is the Image which makes known the paternal Archetype. "The Son is in the Father as the beauty of the image resides in the archetypal form. The Father is in the Son as the archetypal beauty remains in its image, and we must think both these things simultaneously."[2]

The Son is the image of the Father, the Holy Spirit is the image of the Son. Just as the Son reveals the Father, no one can say Jesus is Lord except in the Holy Spirit and so, wrote St. John Damascene, it is in the Holy Spirit that we know Christ as Son of God and God, and it is by the Son that we see the Father. This is the self-manifesting action of the divine persons to which corresponds the ancient doxology: Glory be to the Father, through the Son, in the Holy Spirit.

In such a theology of the image the Father's *monarchy* is always preserved and so the attribute of wisdom, for example, will have the Father as the source of wisdom, the Son as wisdom personified, and the Holy Spirit as the energetic radiance of wisdom common to the three persons and manifested outwardly as gift to men and women. Lossky thought that a proper understanding of the image in trinitarian theology could help us to grasp the often baffling theory of divine energies in the Byzantine theology of the fourteenth century. As mentioned already Gregory Palamas distinguished between the nature of God which is unknowable and the energies proper to and inseparable from God's essence in which He goes forth from Himself and communicates Himself: "The divine and deifying illumination and grace is not the essence but the energy of God," insisted Palamas.[3]

Through the Incarnation the perfect image of God is shown to the world. The image of God hidden in the bosom of the Father from all eternity is now revealed in the flesh. Christ gathers together in Himself all that had gone before and brings to fulfillment that image which was present in the creation of the first man. In fact it was to restore the image lost at the beginning that the Word assumed the flesh in which the created image had been formed. This interpretation dominated the thought of St. Irenaeus, the first eastern theologian (though he eventually became Bishop of Lyons) to explain the work of Christ in terms of the Old Testament doctrine of creation:

"If the Lord had become incarnate in accordance with some different dispensation, and had taken flesh of another substance, he would not then have recapitulated Man in himself, nor indeed could he even have been called flesh. Now, however, this saving Word has become that which actually did exist, namely Man who had perished. And that which had perished possessed flesh and blood. For the Lord, taking clay from the earth, moulded Man; and the whole dispensation of the Lord's coming was on account of this. That is why he himself also possessed flesh and blood, recapitulating in himself not some other, but that original moulding of the Father in his search for that which had perished."[4]

According to Lossky the Eastern Church does not speak of the *imitation* of Christ and prefers the notion of *life in* Christ: union with the Risen Lord is the goal of Christian striving but imitation is not the path to perfection. The way of the Word was one of descent to created being; human effort, on the other hand, must be an ascent, a rising up towards the divine by the grace of the Holy Spirit. Yet with ample quotation from Origen, Maximus the Confessor and Nicholas Cabasilas, Hausherr has shown that the imitation of Christ is indeed a vital strand of eastern spirituality. And so we find the distinction made by Gregory of Nyssa: "The true Christian characteristics are all those which we have been considering about Christ; of these we imitate those qualities of Christ that we are capable of imitating; those other which we are unable to imitate we venerate and adore."[5]

Among creatures Mary, the Mother of God, has most closely imitated the divine perfection of her

Son. She too was filled with the Holy Spirit, raised from death and borne up to heaven. Faithful to the strong oriental tradition of devotion to the *Theotokos*, Gregory Palamas sees Mary as the complete realisation of the beauty of creation: "Wishing to create an image of all beauty, and to manifest clearly to men and to angels the power of His art, God truly created Mary all-beautiful. In her He has brought together all the partial beauties which He distributed amongst other creatures, and has made her the ornament of all beings, visible and invisible; or, rather, He has made her a blessing of all perfections — divine, angelic, and human; a sublime beauty adorning two worlds, lifted up from earth to heaven, and even transcending that."

In spite of their stress on the image of God the Greek writers are watchful in their application of the notion to the actual presence of prayer. They warn against giving any particular image to the Godhead. "In your longing to see the face of the Father in heaven," says Evagrius, "never try to see any shape or form when you are praying. Do not wish to see angels or powers of Christ with your senses or in the end you will become unbalanced, taking the wolf for the shepherd, and worshipping evil spirits." Trying to circumscribe the divine in forms and shapes is the beginning of error and vanity of mind. On the contrary, in freeing itself completely from all imaginations "the spirit receives into itself the characteristics of the deiform image, and becomes clothed with the ineffable beauty of the likeness of the Lord."[6]

From Image to Likeness

"Let us make man according to our image and likeness," decrees Yahweh in the Genesis account of creation. Many of the Greek Fathers interpreted the double simile "image and likeness" not as synonymous but as having entirely different meanings. By his very existence man is in the *image* of God: his life reflects the intellect and will of the divine Word. The *likeness* of God, on the other hand, is the life of grace which begins at baptism and is meant to grow and mature though it can also be lost by sin. Man is the image of God because he is free and he can never lose this image no matter how depraved he may become: he will always have the ability to respond to the Spirit. The likeness of God, however, is an ever-changing reality for it demands a constant effort to be perfect as the heavenly Father is perfect. Thus St. Irenaeus distinguishes between the "image in the flesh," common to all men by the fact of their existence and the "likeness through the Spirit" that, while it is not given at birth, pertains to the full stature of human nature: "The glory of God is man fully alive but the perfect life of man is only found in the vision of God." (This oft-quoted passage frequently loses its second half!)

The beginning of the spiritual life is conversion (*metanoia*). This involves renouncing undisciplined passion and turning to God. Rejection of sin enkindles a different kind of fire in the heart: fervour, longing for and zeal for His glory. For the ascetics of the Christian East the heart is the centre of human life, the root whence flows the whole spiritual life. The heart, said Macarius the Egyptian, is a vessel which contains all the vices but it is also the place where God and the treasures of grace are to be found. "Where grace fills the pastures of the heart, it reigns over all the parts and the thoughts; for there inhabit the intelligence and all thoughts of the soul."[7]

Unless the heart is properly disposed the spirit cannot acquire the likeness of God, that is to say, it cannot become spiritual (*pneumatikos*). This life in the spirit far from being an unconscious development demands a continual custody of the heart through prayer (*theoria*) and action (*praxis*). Without action, wrote St. Maximus, contemplation becomes mere fantasy while action, if it is not inspired by contemplation, is as sterile and as rigid as a statue. Yet the distinction between action and contemplation does not have the same meaning as it carries in the West. For the Orthodox monks the active life consists in purifying the heart by conscious asceticism so that eventually one reaches a state of complete control over the passions (*apatheia*).

The gift of tears, so little understood or appreciated by us, has an important place in eastern spirituality because it is a vital expression of the heart's conversion. "When our soul departs from life we shall not be accused because we have not worked miracles, or have not been theologians, or have not seen visions, but we shall all certainly have to give account before God because we have not wept unceasingly for our sins," warned St. John Climacus, and he spoke of the flow of tears after baptism as even more significant than the water of baptism itself, "though this be a bold saying."[8]

The cry of the repentant publican is the basis of the Jesus Prayer and an abiding sense of sorrow for sin is considered essential at every stage of the spiritual journey. "Weep for your sins, there is no other way to salvation," advised Abbot Pimen and so the plea of the publican must accompany the just even to the gates of the Kingdom. The Byzantine liturgy often quotes the third beatitude (Blessed are they who mourn, they shall be comforted) and sees such tears as a holy gift, a charism of the Spirit and the prelude to infinite joy. This weeping is above all an interior one, cleansing our hearts and enabling us to return to God.

Tears and contrition, then, are the beginning of prayer. Without prayer there can be no union with God. "The power of prayer," stated Gregory Palamas, "fulfills the sacrament of our union with God because it is a bond connecting rational creatures with their Creator." It is more important than even the practice of virtue because without prayer there is little hope of perseverance in good living. Indeed, the greatest of the virtues, love of God, is itself the fruit of prayer: it is through prayer that man enters in to communion with his heavenly Father and realises he is a beloved child.

Christian prayer grows through different stages. At first there is an emphasis on petition but gradually supplication ceases as the soul entrusts itself more and more to the will of God. Pure prayer, contemplation, begins when the mind is wholly turned to God and united in all things with the divine will. One enters a realm of peace and rest (*hesychia*) where all movement of the soul, including prayer itself, fades away. "The mind has ascended here above prayer, and, having found what is more excellent, it desists from prayer." In this state, Isaac the Syrian goes on to say, "nature remains without motion, without action, without the memory of earthly things."[9] A person is then so wrapt in the divine presence that he loses all sense of consciousness and experiences a ravishing of the spirit sometimes called ecstasy (*ekstasis*).

The eastern mystics, like their Carmelite counterparts, are careful to note that such raptures are far from being the final stage of the spiritual life. They are rather only the beginning of contemplation. Symeon the New Theologian compares ecstasy to the excitement of a man emerging from a darkened cell on catching the first glimpse of light. Just as gradually he gets used to the light so the Christian advancing along the path of union leaves ecstasies behind. The real proof of genuine progress is charity towards one's neighbor. "I know a man," wrote St. Symeon, "who desired the salvation of his brethren so fervently that he often besought God with burning tears and with his whole heart, in an excess of zeal worthy of Moses, that, either his brethren might be saved with him, or that he might be condemned with them. For he was bound to them in the Holy Spirit by such a bond of love that he did not even wish to enter the kingdom of heaven if to do so meant being separated from them."[10]

A modern presentation of the ascetical and mystical teaching of Orthodoxy can be found in the writings of Catherine de Hueck Doherty. Born in Russia at the beginning of the century, she left her country after the October Revolution of 1917, and settled in Canada where she started a movement to help the destitute. The religious traditions of the Russian Orthodox Church are dynamically portrayed in her trilogy: *Poustinia*, *Sobornost* and *Strannik*.[11]

In *Poustinia*, the Russian word for desert, Catherine speaks of the need for prayer and how in a quiet, lonely place — be it a room, a shack, or one's heart — people can find the God who dwells within them. *Sobornost* (unity) is a glowing account of that unity first experienced on earth at Pentecost, a unity that reflects the love of the Blessed Trinity and which Christians must strive to construct at every level of life by "forging a chain of hearts."

Through contemplating sobornost in the poustinia the person faithful to prayer receives the invitation to become a pilgrim. This is *Strannik*, the pilgrimage each of us must make to union with God. It is a journey with the Pilgrim Christ where the soles of one's feet become bloody from the sharp stones of men's hearts. "These pilgrims are easily seen because they leave bloody spots along the way. They are easily seen because there is a light coming from those spots. And now those pilgrims who are really pilgrims because God called them to be such pilgrims, having passed through meditating and contemplating sobornost and poustinia, are now making this rhythm — sobornost, poustinia and strannik — their way of life."[12]

Icons

Icons are an indispensable part of Orthodox prayer and worship. Though the word icon (*eikon*: image, portrait) can be used of any representation upon vessels, garments or walls it is especially applied to portable images. The icon is theology in colour and we cannot hope to understand eastern spirituality without an appreciation of its mysticism. It is a summary and compendium of Orthodox piety and so a consideration of icons forms a fitting conclusion to the present work.

It is necessary first of all to emphasise that icons are not religious art in the western sense of the word. They are sacred objects in themselves and are venerated as such both in homes and churches. So strong is this veneration that during the eighth century it provoked a harsh reaction from the iconoclast (image-breaking) emperors. The outstanding defender of images during that crisis, St. Theodore the Studite, compared the Christian artist to God Himself creating man in his image: "The fact that God made man in His image and resemblance shows that iconography is a divine action."[13]

St. John Damascene, who suffered the loss of his right hand in the same persecution, argued that material representations are part of the Christian doctrine of the Incarnation: "From the moment the divinity united itself to our nature, our nature was glorified as by life-giving and wholesome medicine, and received access to incorruptibility: this is why the death of the saints is celebrated, temples are built in their honour, and their images are painted and venerated."[14] In its condemnation of iconoclasm the Second Council of Nicea put icons on an equal level with Sacred Scripture as an instrument of revelation and in 842 a feast proclaiming the legitimacy of icons, The Triumph of Orthodoxy, was introduced into the liturgy and has been commemorated ever since on the first Sunday of Lent. There is a "real presence" of the heavenly Archetype in the icon.

The painting of icons is governed by strict rules. First of all, the artist must be worthy of his high calling. It is unthinkable that he be without faith and a modern commentator on icons, Ouspensky, asks how it could be possible for an atheist or a non-Christian to capture the true meaning and intention of a sacred piece of work: "One does not invite a nonbeliever to preach a sermon, which in fact is of less importance in a church than an icon, just because he happens to be a brilliant orator." The Council of Moscow (1551) spelt out in detail the moral requirements of the iconographer: humility, sobriety, honesty, gentleness and, above all, spiritual and physical purity. The same council is equally emphatic about the necessary competence — those who have not the gift to paint must be forbidden to do so lest their clumsiness become an offence against God. The immediate preparation of the artist consists of prayer and fasting since he will need not only human talent but also the assistance of the Holy Spirit.[15]

The role of the painter is not to discover new techniques or explore fresh models but to follow the guidelines of the ancient masters. The heavenly prototype does not change. Like the preaching of doctrine, to which it is compared by the Second Council of Nicea, the composition of an icon must be in accord with the norms laid down by the Fathers of the Church. The monks, especially those on Mount Athos, are custodians of the art and Symeon of Thessalonica (†1429) illustrates the seriousness of their approach in his instruction: "Teach with words, write with letters, paint with colours, all in conformity with the tradition. Painting is as genuine as the content of the books; it is a work of divine grace because what is represented is holy."[16] It is not surprising, therefore, to find in the liturgical calendar iconographic saints canonised for their artistic endeavours.

The most frequent theme of iconography is the sacred face of the Saviour, the image "made without hands," whose icon is not according to mere human standards but is the very face of God incarnate. Scenes from the Gospel such as the transfiguration (sometimes symbolising contemplation and the inaccessibility of God), the baptism of Christ and the descent into hell are quite common. The Mother of God, *Theotokos*, is another favourite and her icon always has a privileged position on the iconostasis (the veil before the sanctuary on which the icons are hung). Paintings of the saints and angels are also popular and indeed the most original of the icons must surely be the fifteenth century Old Testament Trinity based on the three angels of Genesis by Andrei Rubljev.

An icon is not of course adored as is the Blessed Trinity but, on the other hand, it is not just a holy picture which helps us to meditate. Once blessed it becomes a sacred object to be venerated and honoured, a meeting place between God and man which will inspire us to action. The Orthodox see every icon as "a ray emanating from the unique and indivisible light of God" — it is a particular aspect of the divine presence.[17] Consequently icons are not intended to be sold in shops or become items of trade for they are treated with the same reverential care as the vessels of the altar.

Icons are not meant to be exact portraits but go beyond the physical appearance to the inner, spiritual reality. Like the works of the western El Greco they deliberately ignore the laws of time and space. They are a form of abstract art. Icons have neither volume (the Orthodox reject the use of statues because of what they consider to be a danger of materialisation) nor perspective: Christ, the Virgin and the saints, rather than the spectator, are the centre point around which everything else revolves. Thus they present an inverse perspective which puts the viewer in his proper place; instead of entering the scene from his position he receives from the icon the super-human power flowing within it. An icon "does not exist simply to direct our imagination during our prayers. It is a material centre in which there reposes an energy, a divine force, which unites itself to human art."[18]

Icons point beyond the visible world. They are not intended primarily to be an expression of the artist's feelings (they are generally anonymous and hard to identify) nor even to arouse sentiments of devotion but instead they bring us into the presence of God. This is particularly true of early Greek icons which reflect the power and detachment of the imperial court. Later icons, such as those coming from medieval Russia where Christians were a peasant people suffering oppression from the Tartars, reveal a more tender and consoling piety. Outstanding among the latter is the Madonna of Vladimir from the beginning of the twelfth century.

As with the eucharistic celebration ("the icon of the heavenly liturgy"), icons are not a purely subjective calling to mind of past events but are a real entry into the life of the Incarnate Word. So it is only to be expected that the artist invokes the Spirit and St. Luke (patron of artists as well as doctors) before embarking on his task. The following is an example of such a prayer:

> "Divine Lord of all that exists, you have illumined with your Holy Spirit our apostle and evangelist Luke so that he could represent the beauty of your most holy Mother, the one who held you in her arms when you were small and could say: 'The grace of him who has been born of me is spread throughout the world.' Enlighten and direct my soul, my heart and my spirit. Guide the hands of your unworthy servant so that he may

worthily and perfectly portray your image, that of your Mother and all the saints, for the glory, joy and adornment of your holy Church. Pardon the sins of those who will venerate these images and who, kneeling devoutly before them give homage to those they represent. Protect them from all evil influences and instruct them with good counsel. I ask this through the mediation of your most Holy Mother, the apostle Saint Luke, and all the saints. Amen."[19]

Notes

Part One
1. Quoted from V. Lossky, *The Mystical Theology of the Eastern Church*, London 1957, p. 8.
2. *The Trinity*, London 1970.
3. Lossky, *op. cit.* pp. 64-5.
4. V. Lossky, *In the Image and Likeness of God*, London 1975, p. 13.
5. PG 44, 297-430.
6. *Patrology*, p. 6.
7. Lossky, *Mystical Theology*, pp. 27-31.
8. PG 44, 1000D. Quoted from *From Glory to Glory*, ed. J. Daniélou & H. Musurillo, New York, 1961, p. 247.
9. PG 44, 1001B.
10. *From Glory to Glory*, p. 118.
11. Ibid. p. 270.
12. For what follows cf. Lossky, *In the Image*, pp. 52ff.
13. PG 150, 932D. Quoted from *Mystical Theology*, p. 69.
14. PG 151, 433B. Quoted from *In the Image*, pp. 58-61.
15. *In the Image*, p. 69.
16. M. Fahey, "Orthodox Ecumenism and Theology." *Theological Studies*, Sept. 1978, p. 468.

Part Two

1. J. Meyendorff, *Christ in Eastern Christian Thought*, New York 1975, p. 9.
2. Lossky, *Mystical Theology*, pp. 10-11.
3. *Letter to Nestorius*, Feb. 430.
4. A. Grillmeier, *Christ in Christian Tradition*, London 1965, p. 375.
5. Quoted from Meyendorff, op. cit., p. 157.
6. Quoted from Lossky, *Mystical Theology*, p. 141.
7. Cf. Meyendorff, op. cit. p. 28ff.
8. Lossky, *Mystical Theology*, pp. 149-50.
9. This section is based on J. Jungmann, *The Place of Christ in Liturgical Prayer*, London 1965.
10. Ibid.
11. Quoted from G. Maloney, *The Breath of the Mystic*, New Jersey 1974, pp. 90-91.
12. Cf. P. Adnes, "Prière à Jésus" in *Dict. de. Spir.*
13. *Living Prayer*, London 1966, pp. 87-88.

Part Three

1. Cf. P. Evdokimov, *L'Espirit Saint dans La Tradition Orthodox*, Paris 1969, p. 60.
2. Lossky, *Mystical Theology*, pp. 159-60.
3. Ibid. p. 161.
4. Cf. J. Meyendorff, *Byzantine Theology*, London 1975, p. 168.
5. Cf. Evdokimov, op. cit. pp. 48-78.
6. Cf. *In the Image*, pp. 72ff.
7. *L'Espirit Saint*, p. 76.
8. Quoted from *Mystical Theology*, pp. 160-1.
9. Ibid. pp. 163, 170.
10. Ibid. pp. 171-2.

11. P. Hammond, *The Waters of Marah: The Present State of the Greek Church*. London 1956, pp. 20-1.
12. Cf. B. Bobrinskoy, "Liturgies Orientales" in *Dict. de Spir.* cols. 915-923.
13. Ibid.
14. Evdokimov, op. cit. pp. 100-6.
15. Contakion of Pentecost. Quoted from Meyendorff, *Byzantine Theology*, p. 173ff.
16. Cf. Bobrinskoy, op. cit. col. 923.

Part Four

1. Quoted from Lossky, *In the Image*, p. 126.
2. Gregory of Nyssa, quoted from Lossky, *In the Image*, p. 134.
3. *Mystical Theology*, p. 70.
4. Cf. J. Danielou, *Gospel Message and Hellenistic Culture* pp. 166-83, 398-408.
5. Quoted from Maloney, *The Breath of the Mystic*, p. 118. Cf. I. Hausherr, *Études de Spiritualité Orientale*, Rome 1969, pp. 217-45.
6. Quoted from *Mystical Theology*, p. 194, p. 217.
7. Ibid. pp. 211-2.
8. Ibid. pp. 201-205.
9. Ibid. pp. 207-8.
10. Ibid. p. 214.
11. All published by the Ave Maria Press, U.S.A.
12. *Strannik*, p. 24.
13. Quoted from Meyendorff, *Christ in Eastern Christian Thought*, p. 190.
14. Ibid. p. 191.
15. Cf. "Incone" in *Dict. de Spir.* col. 1229-31.
16. Ibid. col. 1227.
17. Cf. *The Year of Grace of the Lord*, Oxford 1980, p. 133.

18. Lossky, *The Mystical Theology*, p. 189.
19. P. Miquel, "Incone," in *Dict. de Spir*. cols. 1229-1237. I am also indebted to Fr. P. O'Connell, S.J. for his suggestions on icons and other helpful comments on Orthodox spirituality.

SPIRITUAL DIRECTION
Contemporary Readings   5.95

Edited by: Kevin Culligan, O.C.D. The revitalized ministry of
spiritual direction is one of the surest signs of renewal in today's Church. In this book seventeen leading writers and
spiritual directors discuss history, meaning, demands and
practice of this ministry. Readers of the book should include
not just the spiritual elite, but the entire Church — men and
women, clergy and laity, members of religious communities.

THE RETURNING SUN
Hope for a Broken World   2.50

George A. Maloney, S.J. In this collection of meditations, the
author draws on his own experiences rooted in Eastern Christianity to aid the reader to enter into the world of the "heart." It
is hoped that through contemplation of this material he/she
will discover the return of the inextinguishable Sun of the
universe, Jesus Christ, in a new and more experiential way.

LIVING HERE AND HEREAFTER
Christian Dying, Death and Resurrection   2.95

Msgr. David E. Rosage. The author offers great comfort to us
by dispelling our fears and anxieties about our life after this
earthly sojourn. Based on God's Word as presented in Sacred
Scripture, these brief daily meditations help us understand
more clearly and deeply the meaning of suffering and death.

PRAYING WITH SCRIPTURE IN THE HOLY LAND:
Daily Meditations With the Risen Jesus   2.95

Msgr. David E. Rosage. Herein is offered a daily meeting with the Risen Jesus in those Holy Places which He sanctified by His human presence. Three hundred and sixty-five Scripture texts are selected and blended with the pilgrimage experiences of the author, a retreat master, and well-known writer on prayer.

DISCERNMENT:
Seeking God in Every Situation   3.50

Rev. Chris Aridas. "Many Christians struggle with ways to seek, know and understand God's plan for their lives. This book is prayerful, refreshing and very practical for daily application. It is one to be read and used regularly, not just read." *Ray Roh, O.S.B.*

A DESERT PLACE   1.95

Adolfo Quezada. "The author speaks of the desert place deep within, where one can share the joy of the Lord's presence, but also the pain of the nights of our own faithlessness." *Pecos Benedictine.*

MOURNING: THE HEALING JOURNEY   2.50

Rev. Kenneth J. Zanca. Comfort for those who have lost a loved one. Out of the grief suffered in the loss of both parents within two months, this young priest has written a sensitive, sympathetic yet humanly constructive book to help others who have lost loved ones. This is a book that might be given to the newly bereaved.

THE BORN-AGAIN CATHOLIC   3.50

Albert H. Boudreau. This book presents an authoritative im-
primatur treatment of today's most interesting religious issue.
The author, a Catholic layman, looks at Church tradition past
and present and shows that the born-again experience is not
only valid, but actually is Catholic Christianity at its best. The
exciting experience is not only investigated, but the reader is
guided into revitalizing his or her own Christian experience.
The informal style, colorful personal experiences, and helpful
diagrams make this book enjoyable and profitable reading.

WISDOM INSTRUCTS HER CHILDREN:
The Power of the Spirit and the Word   3.50

John Randall, S.T.D. The author believes that now is God's
time for "Wisdom." Through the Holy Spirit, "power" has
become much more accessible in the Church. Wisdom, however, lags behind and the result is imbalance and disarray. The
Spirit is now seeking to pour forth a wisdom we never dreamed
possible. This outpouring could lead us into a new age of
Jesus Christ! This is a badly needed, most important book, not
only for the Charismatic Renewal, but for the whole Church.

DISCOVERING PATHWAYS TO PRAYER   2.95

Msgr. David E. Rosage. Following Jesus was never meant to be
dull, or worse, just duty-filled. Those who would aspire to a life
of prayer and those who have already begun, will find this book
amazingly thorough in its scripture-punctuated approach.

"A simple but profound book which explains the many ways
and forms of prayer by which the person hungering for closer
union with God may find Him." *Emmanuel Spillane, O.C.S.O.,
Abbot, Our Lady of the Holy Trinity Abbey, Huntsville, Utah.*

GRAINS OF WHEAT   2.50

Kelly B. Kelly. This little book of words received in prayer is filled with simple yet often profound leadings, exhortations and encouragement for daily living. Within the pages are insights to help one function as a Christian, day by day, minute by minute.

BREAD FOR THE EATING   2.50

Kelly B. Kelly. Sequel to the popular GRAINS OF WHEAT, this small book of words received in prayer draws the reader closer to God through the imagery of wheat being processed into bread. The author shares her love of the natural world.

DESERT SILENCE:
A Way of Prayer for an Unquiet Age   2.50

Alan J. Placa. and *Brendan Riordan.* The pioneering efforts of the men and women of the early church who went out into the desert to find union with the Lord has relevance for those of us today who are seeking the pure uncluttered desert place within to have it filled with the loving silence of God's presence.

WHO IS THIS GOD YOU PRAY TO?   2.50

Bernard Hayes, C.R. Who is God to me? How do I "picture" Him? This book helps us examine our negative images of God and, through prayer, be led to those images which Jesus reveals to us and which can help us grow into a deeper and more valid relationship with God as Father, Lover, Redeemer, etc.

UNION WITH THE LORD IN PRAYER
Beyond Meditation to Affective Prayer Aspiration and Contemplation
1.50

Venard Polusney, O. Carm. "A magnificent piece of work. It touches on all the essential points of Contemplative Prayer. Yet it brings such a sublime subject down to the level of comprehension of the 'man in the street,' and in such an encouraging way."
Abbott James Fox, O.C.S.O. (former superior of Thomas Merton at the Abbey of Gethsemane).

ATTAINING SPIRITUAL MATURITY
FOR CONTEMPLATION
(According to St. John of the Cross)
1.50

Venard Polusney, O. Carm. "I heartily recommend this work with great joy that at last the sublime teachings of St. John of the Cross have been brought down to the understanding of the ordinary Christian without at the same time watering them down. For all (particularly for charismatic Christians) hungry for greater contemplation."
George A. Maloney, S.J. Editor of Diakonia,
Professor of Patristics and Spirituality Fordham University.

THE PRAYER OF LOVE . . .
The Art of Aspiration
1.95

Venard Polusney, O. Carm. "It is the best book I have read which evokes the simple and loving response to remain in love with the Lover. To read it meditatively, to imbibe its message of love, is to have it touch your life and become part of what you are."
Mother Dorothy Guilbuilt, O. Carm., Superior General, Lacombe, La.

PRAYING WITH MARY   2.95

Msgr. David E. Rosage. This book is one avenue which will help us discover ways and means to satisfy our longing for prayer and a more personal knowledge of God. Prayer was Mary's lifestyle. As we come to know more about her life of prayer we will find ourselves imitating her in our approach to God.

LINGER WITH ME
Moments Aside With Jesus   3.50

Rev. Msgr. David E. Rosage. God is calling us to a listening posture in prayer in the desire to experience Him at the very core of our being. Monsignor Rosage helps us to "come by ourselves apart" daily and listen to what Jesus is telling us in Scripture.

THE BOOK OF REVELATION:
What Does It Really Say?   2.50

John Randall, S.T.D. The most discussed book of the Bible today is examined by a scripture expert in relation to much that has been published on the Truth. A simply written and revealing presentation. The basis for many discussion groups.

POOR IN SPIRIT:
Awaiting All From God   1.95

Cardinal Garrone. Not a biography of the Mother Teresa of her age, this spiritual account of Jeanne Jugan's complete and joyful abandonment to God leads us to a vibrant understanding of spiritual and material poverty. Jeanne Jugan was recently beatified.

LIVING FLAME PRESS
Box 74, Locust Valley, N.Y. 11560

QUANTITY

_____	Prayer: The Eastern Tradition — 2.95
_____	Spiritual Direction — 5.95
_____	The Returning Sun — 2.50
_____	Living Here and Hereafter — 2.95
_____	Praying With Scripture in the Holy Land — 2.45
_____	Discernment — 3.50
_____	A Desert Place — 1.95
_____	Mourning: The Healing Journey — 2.50
_____	The Born-Again Catholic — 3.50
_____	Wisdom Instructs Her Children — 3.50
_____	Discovering Pathways to Prayer — 2.95
_____	Grains of Wheat — 2.50
_____	Bread for the Eating — 2.50
_____	Desert Silence — 2.50
_____	Who Is This God You Pray To — 2.50
_____	Union With the Lord in Prayer — 1.50
_____	Attaining Spiritual Maturity — 1.50
_____	The Prayer of Love — 1.95
_____	Praying With Mary — 3.50
_____	Linger With Me — 3.50
_____	The Book of Revelation — 2.50
_____	Linger With Me — 3.50
_____	Poor in Spirit — 1.95
_____	Enfolded by Christ — 2.50

NAME_____

ADDRESS _____

CITY_____ STATE_____ ZIP _____

Payment enclosed. Kindly include $.70 postage and handling on orders up to $5; $1.00 on orders up to $10; more than $10 but less than $50 add 10% of total; over $50 add 8% of total. Canadian residents add 20% exchange rate, plus postage and handling.